S0-ARO-730

**COMBATING SPIRITUAL
STRONGHOLDS SERIES**

Overcoming
Confusion

by
Rick Joyner

MorningStar Publications
A DIVISION OF MORNINGSTAR FELLOWSHIP CHURCH
P.O. Box 440
Wilkesboro, NC 28697

Published by MorningStar Publications, a division of MorningStar Fellowship Church

International Standard Book Number 1-929371-26-8.

Overcoming Confusion

Chapter One

Understanding Confusion

Confusion is one of the most devastating enemies of truth and of human achievement. Confusion can cripple the most brilliant or the most diligent. For this reason getting free from confusion can make one of the most radical changes in a person's life, changing it from one of defeat and depression into a life filled with joy, peace, and fruitfulness. Therefore, recognizing and overcoming the spirit of confusion is essential for all who will walk in their destiny and accomplish their purpose.

Living with confusion is like being in a thick fog every day. Many become so accustomed to this that they do not even know they are living in a state of confusion. Like children with poor eyesight who put on glasses for the first time, they are astonished at the world around them when they break out from under this terrible oppression. As Proverbs 4:18 states, **"But the path of the righteous is like the light of dawn, that shines brighter and brighter until the full day."** Therefore, Christians should live by a light in their life that gets brighter every day. If this is not the case for you, then there is a good possibility that in some way you have departed from the path that you were called to walk, and by this opened the door to confusion.

However, you can be encouraged because this can be corrected almost as quickly as the child with poor eyesight puts on a pair of prescription glasses. Just as this child will immediately see the world differently, when you break the power of confusion off of your life, you too will start to see the world so clearly that you will immediately begin to live with a new decisiveness, confidence, and peace that others will probably see as miraculous. As a Christian you are not called to live in confusion, but to walk in a light that not only makes your own path clear, but also reveals the path of light to others who are walking in darkness. You must not settle for anything less.

I live on a mountain because I like to be in a place of vision. On a clear day I can see mountain ranges that are nearly one hundred miles away. It is especially beautiful when there is fog in the valley and I can look down on a blanket of white below while standing in bright sunshine. This is the way we are called to live as Christians—in a place of clear vision above the fog and confusion that is in the world.

If you have ever been in a fog as it begins to burn away, you know that it starts by getting brighter as the sun thins the cloud above you. Then, when the shafts of light begin to break through, you know it will not be long before the fog is completely burned away. In a short period of time your perspective can go from a few feet to a very long distance. This is what happens when people are delivered from confusion—they are amazed at how far they can suddenly begin to see.

The Sonlight of Understanding

The very title of this chapter, "Understanding Confusion," may seem like an oxymoron. However, it is precisely what one must do to defeat confusion. Understanding it is the biggest part of the battle to overcoming it. Understanding brings light, and light casts out darkness. When you open your shades at night, darkness does not flow into your house, but rather the light flows out into the darkness. This is because light is more powerful than darkness, and will always overcome it. So we will begin this study by shining the light of understanding with a basic definition of confusion. Then we will seek to expand this definition, and our understanding, until there is no place left for it to hide in our lives.

The dictionary defines *confuse* "to make mentally uncertain, to jumble." For the purpose of this study we will define confusion as *a spiritual or mental stronghold that prevents clear thinking and understanding.* The cause of confusion can be physical, such as chemical imbalances in the body that affect our mental activity and clarity. When it is the result of a physical problem, it can usually be overcome with such things as diet and exercise. However, the root of this problem is usually spiritual and is a very real "living" enemy that has a mind of its own, and a strategy that it is using against us. Just recognizing it as a problem can illuminate its strategy and begin to unravel its web in our lives.

Obviously confusion can range in power and degree. It can keep us from understanding a single matter clearly or become so pervasive that it keeps us from understanding almost anything clearly. Even if our state of confusion seems relatively mild we must resolve that we are not going to allow any of it in our lives. Once confusion gets a foothold into just one part of our lives it will begin to undermine our faith, confidence, and eventually spill over into other areas. Its goal is the complete disruption of our lives. It wants to hinder our progress in everything. If it is not cut off at its root, like a weed it will come back and multiply. This is why our goal must be to understand the roots of confusion, and learn to pull it out by its roots so that it cannot come back or spread.

Regardless of how pervasively confusion grips your life, you can be sure that you can be *completely* free from it. That is the goal of this book—to help you get completely free of confusion so that in place of the clouds and gloom you will walk every day in increasing light. If we are on the path that He has called us to, the light in our life will grow brighter every day! We must never settle for less than this, and never allow the enemy to rob us of this basic gift from God to His children—light!

Symptoms of Confusion

One of the first effects of confusion is to cause us to live in an increasing state of hesitancy. If it is not recognized and over-come, it will grow into a stronghold of fear, depression, and hopelessness. Christians should never be in any of these mental states, so if we are subject to them to any degree, we have a battle to fight and we can easily win it.

A main goal of confusion is to darken all of our thinking and perceptions so that we will not walk in faith. It usually starts in an area of our life that is very important for what

God is doing with us. For example, we may have great clarity about our job or profession, but be in confusion about how to raise our children, relate to our spouse, or to the church. The effect of this will usually be to gravitate toward the area of our lives where we feel more in control, and then we will begin to drift from the area where we have confusion. In the case sighted above it will compel us to become increasingly devoted to our jobs, and increasingly separated from our families or churches. Therefore confusion is often the beginning of the separations and divisions that destroy relationships. This is almost always a primary strategy of the spirit of confusion—the destruction of relationships.

It is obvious that if the enemy is targeting a relationship, it is usually because of the importance of that relationship. Therefore, we must determine that the area or relationship which is being attacked by confusion is probably very important to our purpose, so we must not let confusion steal it from us. Sometimes relationships in our lives need to change, **"for God is not the author of confusion…" (I Corinthians 14:33 NKJV).** If it is His will for a relationship to change He will not use confusion to do it. We therefore must learn to fight for every area and every relationship that is being attacked by confusion.

The key to keeping confusion out of our relationships is to walk uprightly in them. In Proverbs 4:18, it is **"the path of the righteous"** that gets brighter and brighter. When we allow unrighteousness to enter a relationship we have opened the door wide for confusion, and it will usually bring many evil friends. Therefore, having a clear definition of righteousness is basic to the clarity that overcomes confusion. Compromising biblical standards of morality and integrity will open us to confusion and our relationships to destruction.

We must also keep in mind that almost all human relationships will be difficult at times. When there were just two brothers on the entire earth, they could not get along. Even so, we can have difficulties without having confusion. Dispatching the confusion is usually the first step to overcoming the other problems that may exist in our relationships.

Daylight

The Lord said, **"and you shall know the truth, and the truth shall make you free" (John 8:32)**. The normal Christian life is one of increasing light and clarity because the normal Christian life is one of growing in truth. The purpose of this study is to illuminate the truth about the causes of confusion and to unravel any jumbled thinking, replacing it with truth so that we can clearly see the course that is set before us. A basic goal of our lives should be clarity of thought, because that means the truth is becoming more clear to us. This will enable us to walk with increasing confidence and boldness, as well as to have success in all that we do.

Chapter Two

The Main Entry Gate of Confusion

Though our problems in this world can become very complicated, the way out of them is usually very simple. However, "simple" and "easy" do not necessarily mean the same thing. To be obedient to our callings as Christians is a simple matter, but difficult to do. Even so, it is always ultimately much easier to obey and do what is right than it is not to obey.

Simple obedience to the Lord and living by His Word is the ultimate way out of confusion. Compromising what we know is right is to depart from **"the path of the righteous" (Proverbs 4:18),** and is the biggest open door to confusion in our lives. So our goal must be to know the truth and obey it.

This does not necessarily imply that if we are in confusion we are in disobedience to the Lord, or doing something unrighteous. There are other causes of confusion that we will cover later. However, disobedience to the truth that we know is the most common open door of confusion. If this is the open

13

door to confusion in our lives then it is a simple matter to get rid of it—obey the truth.

If there is unrighteousness in our lives we must honestly and openly admit to it and repent, which means to turn away from it so we can be free of confusion. As we are told in I John 1:9, **"If we confess our sins, He is faithful and righteous to forgive us our sins and to cleanse us from all unrighteousness."** As soon as we do this we can expect clarity to come because we have returned to the **"path of the righteous"** which is one of ever increasing light.

Of course this does not mean we will not have problems, but both the nature of any problem and the solution for overcoming it will become increasingly clear to us if we stay on the path. Clarity of vision is fundamental to every life that is on the path of righteousness. Sin and unrighteousness will always blur our vision and open us to confusion. This is why Proverbs 4:19 states, **"The way of the wicked is like darkness; they do not know over what they stumble."**

If unrighteousness is in your life it has probably not only blurred your vision, but made inroads for confusion into other areas of your life as well. That is why I John 1:9 says that if we confess our sins, He will

"...cleanse us from *all* unrighteousness," which will also bring clarity in every area where we have had confusion.

The Strategy

Understanding our enemy, confusion, is the first step to defeating it, and is actually the biggest part of the battle. However, after that we must have resolve to persevere and fight it on every front until it is completely defeated and driven from our lives. In II Kings 13 there is an interesting story that illustrates what we must now resolve to do.

In this story a king of Israel came to the prophet Elisha to inquire as to whether he should go to battle with a certain enemy. Elisha told him to take his bow and arrows and strike the ground. The king did this three times. The prophet became angry with him, saying that he should have struck the ground five or six times. Because he had only struck it three times he would only defeat his enemy three times. Such prophetic antics may be hard to understand, but the point is that when we fight against an enemy we need to strike it as many times as it takes to completely defeat it. If we only partially defeat it we will likely have to continue fighting it for the rest of our lives, for it will keep coming back to us.

There are some principles that we will strike repeatedly in this study. It has been proven that most people need considerable repetition for retention of a thought or idea. It then takes even more repetition to actually change behavior. It is for this reason that recent management studies now recommend that important directives be issued at least four times in writing and verbally to insure compliance. With each repetition the probability of retention is greatly increased. We not only want retention of the truth, but we want to continue repeating it as often as it takes to change our behavior.

If the repetition included in this study is not enough, reread the booklet until your victory is complete. You may also want to reread it periodically just to be sure that certain things have not crept back in. Whenever we cast the enemy out of our life, he does try to return (see Matthew 12:43-45). Our goal is first to get free—then to stay free!

As you may have already concluded, our keynote verse for being delivered from confusion is Proverbs 4:18. It is one of our "arrows" that we are going to keep striking the ground with until we have the total victory. Other arrows are verses that follow in Proverbs 4:18, so lets take the time to read over them carefully here:

But the path of the righteous is like the light of dawn, that shines brighter and brighter until the full day.

The way of the wicked is like darkness; they do not know over what they stumble.

My son, give attention to my words; incline your ear to my sayings.

Do not let them depart from your sight; keep them in the midst of your heart.

For they are life to those who find them, and health to all their whole body.

Watch over your heart with all diligence, for from it flow the springs of life.

Put away from you a deceitful mouth, and put devious lips far from you.

Let your eyes look directly ahead, and let your gaze be fixed straight in front of you.

Watch the path of your feet, and all your ways will be established.

Do not turn to the right nor to the left; turn your foot from evil (Proverbs 4:18-27).

If you are in a battle with confusion, I recommend that you read this text every day for a while, endeavoring to walk in the truth stated herein. Keep beating the ground with these arrows until you have completely defeated your enemy—confusion.

Chapter Three
A Fortress of Truth

Crucial to walking in the light so that your life is devoid of confusion is walking in sound, biblical truth. One of the biblical texts that explains how this is done is Matthew 16:13-18:

Now when Jesus came into the district of Caesarea Philippi, He began asking His disciples, saying, "Who do people say that the Son of Man is?"

And they said, "Some say John the Baptist; and others, Elijah; but still others, Jeremiah, or one of the prophets."

He said to them, "But who do you say that I am?"

And Simon Peter answered and said, "Thou art the Christ, the Son of the living God."

And Jesus answered and said to him, "Blessed are you, Simon Barjona, because flesh and blood did not reveal this to you, but My Father who is in heaven.

And I also say to you that you are Peter, and upon this rock I will build My church; and the gates of Hades shall not overpower it.

Some have interpreted this to mean that Peter is the rock that the Lord is building His church on, but a closer examination of this text reveals otherwise. The Greek word that is translated "Peter" is *Petros* which means a piece of rock, or a stone. The Greek word that is translated "rock" in this text is *Petra*, which is actually a feminine version that literally means "a mass of rock." The rock that the church is being built upon which the gates of hell cannot prevail against is the revelation from the Father of who Jesus is.

No one can come to the Son unless the Father draws him (see John 6:44). It is the revelation from above which is the rock that all true faith must be built on if it is to stand against the storms that will surely come against it. Ideals and intellectual conclusions can be stolen from us, but when the Father Himself reveals a matter, it is a rock in our life that cannot be easily moved. So it is not persuasive arguments from men that lead to true faith—it must be a revelation from the Father of who Jesus is. We are dependent on the Holy Spirit, whom the Father has sent to testify of the Son, for all true illumination.

This is why the apostle John wrote in I John 2:27, **"...His anointing teaches you about all things..."** Even though I obviously believe the principles in this study are true, I know they will accomplish nothing unless the reading of them is accompanied by the Holy Spirit who anoints your study. He was sent to lead us into "all truth," and His anointing is absolutely required for the impartation of spiritual truth.

The fall, and all of our human problems are basically the result of man trying to live without God. The very nature of our redemption should teach us that we need God for everything, especially understanding. For this reason it is not enough for us to just read and try to understand the principles of this book. We must do it in fellowship with the Lord, praying and seeking His help every step of the way. The ultimate deliverance from confusion is to live in His light.

For this reason the Lord is likewise saying to each of us **"Blessed are *you*, (*insert your name here*), because flesh and blood did not reveal this to you, but My Father who is in heaven...and upon this rock (*revelation that comes from the Father*) I will build My church; and the gates of Hades shall not overpower it" (Matthew 16:17-18).** If we have perceived who Jesus is, it is a blessing, a gift, and not our own achievement. When we receive a revelation from the Father, it is also a rock that no amount of human pressure or persuasion can steal from us. This does not mean that all of hell will not try, but faith built on this rock will stand and prevail.

The fortress that we have as a bastion against confusion or any other assault from hell is a revelation of who Jesus is. He is above all rule, authority, and dominion. He has prevailed over sin and the devil, and to the degree that we abide in Him and keep our faith in Him we too will prevail.

Some have wrongly tried to build their lives on a faith in *their* faith instead of faith in who Jesus is. Our faith is not to be in our faith, but in the person of Jesus Christ—who He is and what He has already accomplished for us. Walking in the light is to walk with *The Light*, Jesus.

Knowing Your Shepherd

In John 10:4 the Lord said concerning Himself as the Good Shepherd, **"When he puts forth all his own, he goes before them, and the sheep follow him because they know his voice."** It is clear in this verse that if we are His sheep we will know His voice. We follow Him because we know His voice.

It could be said that we follow Him to the degree that we know His voice. One of the devil's most effective ploys has been to make the very concept of how to know the will of the Lord a confusing issue to many Christians. Therefore, we must address this if we are to be free from confusion.

Even though the matter of knowing the Lord's voice has been confusing to many, it is a relatively simple matter. Most of the confusion around this is the result of the enemy being able to complicate it. How simple is it? How many people can you recognize by looking at their hand, their foot, or any other part of the body? There are basically two things by which we recognize others—their faces and their voices. The same is true with the Lord. We must therefore seek His face and know His voice.

I could pick my wife's voice out of any crowd. I can do this because we have been together so much that I know her voice and can easily distinguish it from any other. The same is the key to knowing the Lord's voice—simply by spending time with Him. The increasing light that is the path of the righteous is an increasing revelation of the Son of God. As we behold His glory more and more, we too are changed into His same image, as we are told in II Corinthians 3:18:

But we all, with unveiled face beholding as in a mirror the glory of the Lord, are being transformed into the same image from glory to glory, just as from the Lord, the Spirit.

It is not enough to just see His glory and to be changed into His same image—we must see His glory with **"an unveiled face."** Confusion is what places many of the veils upon our faces so that His glory is distorted when we behold it, and therefore we are changed into a distorted image of Him. This is the primary reason why so many Christians are so un-Christlike. As we proceed we will try to define and then strip away the veils that are clouding the vision of so many.

Chapter Four

The Complications of the Devil vs. The Simplicity of Devotion to Christ

Besides over-complicating how we recognize the Lord's voice, a primary strategy of the devil is to overly complicate everything that he can. This is a primary way that he spreads confusion. Complication and confusion are co-workers in the devil's strategy. Therefore, we must heed the warning of II Corinthians 11:3:

> **But I am afraid, lest as the serpent deceived Eve by his craftiness, your minds should be led astray from the simplicity and purity of devotion to Christ.**

The words **"led astray"** in this verse are sometimes translated "beguiled," or "bewitched." It is no accident that witchcraft is a complicated hodgepodge of patterns, formulas, and incantations. This is the way the devil likes to be sought, and he will usually only give his power to those who are willing to jump through all of the hoops. It is exactly contrary to the simplicity of how God is approached—simple faith in the Son of God will usher you right into His presence.

As the verse above implies, pure devotion to the Lord is a primary antidote to the way the enemy seeks to lead our minds astray, for which his primary weapon is confusion. To the degree that we keep our devotion to Him simple and pure, confusion will find no place in our lives.

We should also note here that Eve was led astray by the serpent's "craftiness." Craftiness could be defined as a tendency to bend the rules and get away with it. If that kind of mentality is in our lives it will likely become a stronghold for confusion to enter. This tendency will greatly complicate our lives with many confusing problems. If our goal is anything but pure obedience—pure devotion to Christ, we will be open to confusion. We should therefore not want to bend the rules, or seek to push them to their limits, but rather to know them so we can obey them.

The devil caused the first fall by getting Eve to question God. He asked her a simple question, "Did God really say that?" The first step toward a fall and confusion is simply to begin questioning the clear directives of God. This was the devil's strategy to complicate something that God had made very simple—"Don't do it."

After the serpent saw that Eve was open to questioning something God had made clear, it was not hard for him to push her further to begin questioning God's motives. Then it was easy for him to goad her into looking at what she was missing. When she looked at the fruit of the forbidden tree she wondered why a good God would deny her something that looked so good. She obviously concluded that He did not really love them, or He did not mean what He said. This line of questioning led to the first fall, and many, many more since.

The point is that we are opening a door wide to deception when we question the clear commands of the Lord or His intentions. This does not mean that we cannot ask Him questions or wonder why. However, there is a big difference between asking because we want to obey Him and asking questions because we want to disobey. If we are going to stay on the path of righteousness we must settle in our hearts that He is always good, just, righteous, and always has our best interests in mind. He is always wise and He is always right.

The Nature of Love

It is tragic the way that skepticism is now viewed as a foundation for wisdom and necessary for the pursuit of truth. Skepticism is the foundation of a darkened soul, an open door to the devil's heart, and is contrary to faith that is the foundation of a genuine pursuit of truth. In I Corinthians 13:7 we are told that love "**... believes all things, hopes all things...**" This does not mean love is naive or does not see flaws and mistakes. What it does mean is that love looks for the best in others and hopes for the best, not the worst. If you are examining someone, looking for the worst in them, you can be sure that the devil will show it to you and bend it considerably as he does.

You may think that anyone who lives by the mandate of love in I Corinthians 13 will suffer perpetual disappointment and hurt. That is very possible. One thing that few realize, and that every Christian needs to settle in their heart and mind, is that being hurt by others is basic to the call of being a Christian. To live in a way that tries to avoid being hurt will divert us from our basic calling and the path of righteousness.

One of the greatest demonstrations of true love is to continue believing in someone after they have disappointed you or hurt you. We are called to take up our crosses daily. The cross is the symbol of the greatest injustice that the world has ever witnessed. No one ever deserved the persecution and death that He suffered less than Jesus did.

Yet, He came into this world knowing that this was going to happen, and willingly went to the cross for our salvation. He said in John 17:18 concerning those whom He had called, **"As Thou didst send Me into the world, I also have sent them into the world."** We have actually been sent into the world to experience injustice and yet, like our Savior, keep on loving and believing in people.

How many of us would earnestly desire to have one more meal with our closest friends if we knew that within hours the same ones in whom we have invested so much, would even deny that they knew us? It is the basic nature of love to love regardless of how those we love return it. This is the way we are also called to walk. This is the Lord who said in Matthew 10:38-39, **"And he who does not take his cross and follow after Me is not worthy of Me. He who has found his life shall lose it, and he who has lost his life for My sake shall find it."**

He does not call us to take up our crosses every day to make atonement for others. His sacrifice alone did that. However, just as He went to the cross and let people hurt Him even though He was completely innocent, doing it for the sake of those who were so unjustly killing Him, we must do the same. We are here to demonstrate the cross by suffering injustice for the sake of the very ones who are treating us unjustly. When we do this in the right spirit, rejoicing that we have been counted worthy to suffer for His name's sake just as the apostles did, rather than feeling sorry for ourselves and walking around with a martyr's complex, the power of the Holy Spirit to bring salvation can be released through us.

Possibly the greatest simplifying factor in our lives would be to let love be our motive in all things in place of the self-seeking and self-interests that usually motivate us. This would so simplify our lives because the Lord promises that if we will seek His interests first, which is His kingdom, He will take care of everything that concerns us, just as He promises in Matthew 6:31-34:

"Do not be anxious then, saying, 'What shall we eat?' or 'What shall we drink?' or 'With what shall we clothe ourselves?'

"For all these things the Gentiles eagerly seek; for your heavenly Father knows that you need all these things.

"But seek first His kingdom and His righteousness; and all these things shall be added to you.

"Therefore do not be anxious for tomorrow; for tomorrow will care for itself. Each day has enough trouble of its own."

One of the greatest sources of anxiety and confusion is our over-concern about the future of our own self-interests. The Lord promises that if we will put the seeking of His kingdom first, He will take care of everything for us. This alone can be one of the biggest de-confusing factors in our lives.

Even though we are here to be hurt and suffer injustice at times, there is a way to do this and actually not be hurt. In fact, that is the way it is supposed to be. How can we be treated unjustly, or hurt by others and not feel it? We are called to be dead to this world. How can a dead man feel hurt or injustice? For us to take up our crosses daily means that we die daily. We accept that all things happening to us are for our good just as we are promised in the Scriptures, so we should rejoice in all of our trials.

You may say that is certainly easier said than done, but I would say that it is easier done than not doing it. The more dead we are the easier our lives will be! Sounds crazy, but it is a sober, profound, truth. If our lives are not easy it is because we have not died to the world yet. In this way we are still seeking to save our lives, but those who lose their lives for His sake will find true life. One issue that we need to settle is that the Lord is not just trying to change us—He is trying to kill us!

To encourage you a little more, the two most powerful beings in the universe are both trying to kill you! God and the devil both want you dead! However, they have different ways of doing it, and for different reasons. God is trying to set you free and give you more life than you can even imagine, while the devil is trying to shackle you in every way he can so he can steal your life. If you let God do it you will be resurrected to a life of more glory and power than you can even imagine—and you will begin to partake of that resurrection power in this life!

There is also no greater freedom that we can ever know than to be dead to this world. What can you do to a dead man? It is impossible for a dead man to be offended, to feel rejected, to feel sorry for himself, or to even get angry. It is impossible for a dead man to be confused. If these things are still happening to us it is only evidence that we have refused to walk in our most basic calling as Christians—to take up our crosses and follow Him.

It is amazing how clear everything becomes when we are dead! If we are dead all of the confusion caused by our selfish ambitions, pride, and secret desire to sin, vanishes. The greatest open door for the clarity of the Spirit of God is the cross.

Chapter Five

The Fear of Man and Confusion

In this chapter we are going to study another main gateway of confusion into our lives—living by the fear of man instead of by the fear of the Lord.

When I speak of the "fear of man" here I am speaking of an inordinate fear of man. By this we recognize that there is a proper respect that we should have for others. The proper respect for others is what we are exhorted to give in Romans 13:7, **"Render to all what is due them: tax to whom tax is due; custom to whom custom; fear to whom fear; honor to whom honor."**

Believe it or not, the Greek word that is translated "fear" in this text actually means *fear!* It could have been translated "alarm" or "fright." There is respect for authority, for the elderly, etc. that we should have. So when I am speaking of "the fear of man," I am speaking of an *inordinate* fear of man.

As we addressed in the last chapter, a great deal of the confusion in people's lives can be broken quickly by the resolve to live in the simplicity of pleasing God rather than other people. When we live by the fear of man instead of the fear of the Lord we put ourselves into the caldron of confusion which is constantly stirred by the whims of others, or the fears empowered by our own constantly changing perceptions of what we think others think of us.

In general, people are not consistent or stable enough for us to put this kind of trust in them. In fact, the whole fallen world is in the grip of every confusion that we resolve to be free from. Therefore, we must begin by freeing ourselves from the world's controls and expectations in every way that it wrongly influences our lives and perceptions.

On the other hand, the Lord has made it very clear what He thinks and expects of us. We can add to this the assurance that He never changes. To live in the fear of the Lord rather than by the fear of man will dispel most of the confusion that afflicts almost every person.

The Confusion of Human Relations

No parents are perfect and at times even the best can do things that confuse their children. There are times when children may do something that irritates their parents and they get a strong reaction from them. The very next day they may do the same thing, but because their parents are in a different mood, they may not get a reaction at all, thereby producing confusion in their lives. It is like trying to play a game when someone is constantly changing the rules and not telling you about it. If confusion or inconsistency is in you, it will come out in your relationships with your children, your spouse, your co-workers, and everyone else. However, we are all this way until we have been perfected in Christ, and I have yet to meet anyone who has fully attained this. Therefore, we must all learn to live in the love that **"covers a multitude of sins,"** forgiving inconsistencies in others just as they are having to forgive ours.

We are all in the process of being delivered from the confusion of this world. We should not allow bad days or bad actions of others to ruin our relationships with them. We should also always be thankful that our Father in heaven is not like us—He never changes and He is working with us to help us to become like Him, which should be our primary goal in life.

There are other causes of confusion that we will address, but the fear of man is certainly one of the most common. It may seem too simplistic now, but the answer to every question we will address in this study will ultimately be to return to the simplicity of devotion to the Lord. Understanding how we allow other people or influences to eclipse our devotion to Him and doing His will, and then understanding how we return to the Lord by repentance, is the path to deliverance from confusion, and even more importantly, sin. If we could live our lives only being concerned with what the Lord thinks of us and not what other people think of us, confusion would have very little access in our lives.

However, we must relate to other people even before we are completely delivered from our fears and the confusion they cause. We need to understand that these relationships are a primary tool that the Lord is using to deliver us. He wants us to love others, but the more we love them the more they can have influence over us. However, we are called to love others much more, while allowing them to control us less. How can we do this?

Basically, we have to do it by not letting other people's expectations control us, as we are told in II Corinthians 5:14, **"For the love of Christ controls us..."** How different would our lives be if we were controlled by the love of Christ? This means loving Him and allowing His love to flow through us. Not only would our lives become far more simple than they are now, but they would also be much more successful because **"love never fails..." (I Corinthians 13:8).**

However, we must realize that this perfect love of Christ actually casts out all fear, even the fear of man, so that we are not controlled by the expectations or desires of those whom we love. It is because of not understanding this one thing that many people who enter into ministry are so quickly burned out—they start taking people's yokes instead of the Lord's yoke. Love is not the permission to control. Perfect love cannot be controlled by anyone but God who alone is perfect.

The Ditch on the Other Side

There is a ditch on either side of the path of life. Many who have fallen into a ditch oversteer when trying to return to the path and end up in the opposite ditch. Repentance often means a radical change of direction, but let us be careful not to over-correct. Now let us return to the statements made in the paragraph above and try to respond to them without making an over-correction.

Does this mean we do not have to respond to human needs? Does this mean we do not respond even to the needs of those we love and who love us? Yes, in fact it does. First, it is not true love if it is controlling or demanding.

Second, we cannot really help anyone, and may even contribute to their sins, confusion, or self-pity, with our human compassion. If we really want to help someone we must do it by God's Spirit. This does not mean that God cannot use us to respond to the needs of others, but we must be led by Him to do it or we will be consumed by trying to respond to the needs of others in our own strength.

Jesus never responded to human needs—He only did what He saw the Father doing. If He sent us out just as He was sent, it also means that we are supposed to live this same way. We are not called to feed all of the hungry, but to feed the hungry that He wants us to feed. He does not send us out to heal all of the sick—He did not even do that. He wants us to heal the sick that He wants us to heal.

Now you may be thinking that this might give many people the license not to respond to other people's needs at all. It is likely that many will take it to that extreme. As Peter said of Paul's teachings, the unstable and untaught distort them. This will always be the case. However, my point about not responding to human needs is not to turn our backs on those in need, as James warned us against, but rather to seek to follow the Lord in our ministry to others, not the wants or expectations of others.

When Jesus told His disciples who were looking at five thousand hungry people, "You give them something to eat," He empowered them to do it, multiplying their resources. When He directs us to meet anyone's needs He will empower us to do it, and when He does we can count on our resources going a lot farther than had we tried to do it on our own.

Of course, many are asking how to know which ones the Lord is leading us to help. Simply—we have to know His voice. Remember, His sheep **"follow Him because they know His voice" (John 10:4).** Getting to know His voice is not complicated. It is based on simply spending time with Him.

Let us also understand that when we determine to not be controlled by other people's expectations, but rather by the love of Christ, this does not mean we rebel against our boss. We must endeavor to live by Colossians 3:23-24: **"Whatever you do, do your work heartily, as for the Lord rather than for men; knowing that from the Lord you will receive the reward of the inheritance. It is the Lord Christ whom you serve."** If we have made the commitment to take a job, we will therefore seek in every way to do the best possible job because of our love for the Lord whom we are ultimately working for, and because of the love that He has given to us for the people we work for and with as well.

If we love others we will also be understanding of why they may not react to us with consistency. We will have an understanding of the confusion in this world that they are having to constantly battle. We will therefore endeavor to be consistent in our relationship to them whether they are or not. This we do because of our love for them, and love will love whether it is rewarded or not. Therefore our goal in all of our relationships should be the simplicity of love that does not waver, even when it is at times rejected or hurt.

As we begin to walk in the consistency that comes from following the One in whom there is no inconsistency or shadow of turning, we will become rocks of refuge in the midst of the storms of confusion in this world. Others will trust us more and more, and this trust can become a bridge by which we can help them to find deliverance through Christ. We must also consider that the more confusion and inconsistency we are faced with in a relationship, the greater the opportunity we have to demonstrate the love of God that does not waver.

Chapter Six
Good Fear and Bad Fear

If we are living by the pure and holy fear of the Lord, we will not fear anything else on this earth. If we live by the fear of the Lord, we will not be controlled by the fear of man or any other fear. When we are not controlled by the fear of man we can give all men the honor and respect that is due them, which is a biblical command, but we will do it with the grace and dignity that is befitting the sons and daughters of the King of kings.

I have learned to be wary of those who give too much honor to men, and those who do not give honor to whom honor is due, as we are commanded in Romans 13:7. Those who refuse to do the latter often claim that they are not going to worship men or live by the fear of man. I obviously agree that we should not do this, but this does not mean we do not give the respect and honor to others that is due. In fact, one of the primary ways we honor the Lord is by honoring others to whom He has delegated His authority.

Those who go to the extreme of refusing to give any honor to those who deserve it are either immature in their faith, lacking in understanding, or they are some of the most dangerous people of all because of the pride that is controlling them. You will find that these are often the very people who actually demand the most respect and honor from others, and will also be the most prone to control and dominate in their relationships with others.

I am not a very formal person. I really don't even like to be called "pastor," much less "apostle," "prophet" or "bishop." I ask everyone in our congregations to call me "Rick" and even my own children do at times. However, I appreciate someone calling me by whatever title they think is appropriate until I tell them otherwise. As a leader with a certain amount of influence I have learned to be wary of those who show me too much respect, and those who do not show me enough. Both are usually going to be a problem. I do not need this respect or acknowledgment. As I said, I don't even tend to like it, but it reveals to me very accurately where a person is spiritually.

When I was in the military we were told not to fraternize with those of lesser rank because they would not respect our authority. That may have been true in the military, and it is also true of what the Lord called the authority of the Gentiles, but it is not true in the kingdom. Jesus not only became close to His disciples, He lived with them. They were right by His side day and night. In the kingdom if someone loses respect for us because they get too close to us something is wrong with *us*. If we are who we claim to be, people should respect us more the closer they get to us.

I want my children and my employees to be completely comfortable and free around me, but I also want them to do what I say the first time I say it. We can and should have both. I may lean toward being too casual, but I am far more alarmed when I see a leader's staff or family having an inordinate fear of him, which is usually demonstrated by a humiliating groveling in his presence. I have learned that those who tend to be the most demanding of having others recognize their title or position are usually the least deserving of that title or position.

One of the most devastating sources of confusion is found in Isaiah 9:16, **"For those who guide this people are leading them astray; and those who are guided by them are brought to confusion."** One does not have to look back far into the history of the church to see that the majority of confusion that has come into the body of Christ has come from leaders who did not walk in righteousness. We will elaborate on this a little more in the next chapter, but for now we must demand the highest standards of morality and integrity from those we recognize as leaders in the church or we will continue to be subject to the terrible confusion that has rested upon the church since the first century. The over concern with titles and positions is a symptom of something basically awry in a person's life, and should be a disqualification from leadership.

It is interesting that the King of kings did not demand anyone to call Him by a title. The ones who have real authority will inevitably be the least demanding of others to recognize it. Those who have true spiritual authority have received it from above, and it is from above that they get their encouragement. Those who know they were sent from above will not be overly encouraged or discouraged by what other people think of them. Those who are inordinately in pursuit of encouragement from the recognition of other men should not be in spiritual leadership. At the same time we must learn to show the proper respect for all of the servants, ambassadors, and leaders the Lord has chosen. We must learn to show the proper respect for others without worshiping or having an inordinate fear of them.

A major open door to confusion will come from trying to serve two masters. This confusion is multiplied when we try to please everyone. Remember, anything with more than one head is a monster. In I Corinthians 11:3 we are told, **"But I want you to understand that Christ is the head of every man..."** Others can be our leaders, have authority and influence with us, but only One can be our Head.

One of the primary ways that confusion enters our lives is when the Lord speaks or leads us in a certain way, and we begin to be concerned about what other people think. Because of this we give honor to others first due to the biblical command, instead of out of respect for the Lord and all authority that He has delegated on the earth.

Whose Ambassador Are You?

In II Corinthians 5:20 Paul wrote, **"Therefore, we are ambassadors for Christ..."** In biblical times to be an ambassador of a nation was the highest honor one could receive from the king or emperor. They did not have phones, fax machines, or email. Because they often could not communicate with their ambassadors for months, only those who were the very best friends of the king, who he knew were of one mind with him and would only represent his interests, would be chosen as an ambassador. Even then ambassadors were recalled every two years because it was felt that after that period of time they would begin to be more sympathetic to the country they were sent to than the one they had been sent from.

Because the Lord does not recall His ambassadors every two years, we must check our hearts continually to be sure that we are representing His interests rather than man's interests. That is why Paul wrote in Galatians 1:10, **"If I were still seeking to please men I would not be a bondservant of Christ."** Think about it. To the degree that we are seeking to please men instead of Christ we will fail to be His bondservant.

In Luke 16:15 the Lord said to the Pharisees, **"You are those who justify yourselves in the sight of men, but God knows your hearts; for that which is highly esteemed among men is detestable in the sight of God."** Consider this—what is highly esteemed among men is detestable in God's sight! I think the reverse is also usually true—that which is highly esteemed with God is detestable in the sight of men. We have a major choice to make in our life. Someone is going to detest what we do— God or men. Who do we want it to be? As the Lord said in Luke 6:26, **"Woe to you** when all men speak well of you, for in the same way their fathers used to treat the false prophets."

Spiritual Adultery

If on your wedding day your future spouse came up to you and said, "Darling, I love you so much that I am going to be faithful to you 364 days a year! I only want one day a year to mess around." Would you go on with the wedding? With that in mind consider James 4:4:

"You adultresses, do you not know that friendship with the world is hostility toward God? Therefore whoever wishes to be a friend of the world makes himself an enemy of God."

We have been betrothed to Christ. We cannot be married to Him and married to the world too. It is not a matter of being mostly His and very seldom mess around with the world—His bride is going to be a pure, chaste virgin, so we cannot determine to be married to the world until He returns and then switch. We have a choice to make. Who are we going to be married to—the world or Christ? It cannot be both. To try to serve both is not only a wide open door to confusion, it is a wide open door to eternal grief.

The Destroyer of Faith

In John 5:44 Jesus asked what should be considered one of the ultimate questions: **"How can you believe when you receive glory from one another and you do not seek the glory that is from the one and only God?"** The Greek word that is translated "glory" here could have been translated "respect," or "honor." Previously, we discussed how we should give respect to those to whom it is due, but here we are profoundly challenged not to seek it from men. As the question implies, to do so is probably the number one destroyer of true faith.

Summary

In I Kings 17:1 we have the dramatic entrance of one of the greatest prophets who ever lived, Elijah. In what appears to have been his first prophetic statement he declares what was probably the main reason why he was trusted with so much authority when he said, **"...As the LORD, the God of Israel lives, before whom I stand..."** Even though Elijah was standing before the king at the time, it was the Lord that he was really standing before. It was the Lord, not men, not even the king, who Elijah lived his life before. To the degree that we can do this we will be delivered from confusion, and can be trusted with real authority.

Again, normal Christianity is a life of ever increasing light, peace, and joy. We must resolve that we will not continue to settle for anything less than the joy and peace which is the inheritance of every citizen of the kingdom of God.

It is not normal for a Christian to be in confusion. Christ is the **"light of the world" (John 8:12)**. How can we be in confusion if we are abiding in Him? We must recognize confusion as evidence that we have either been distracted from our place in Him, or are under an assault of the enemy that intends to do just that—so our options are to repent or fight. The purpose of the remainder of this study is to help us determine which it should be, and how to do either one when it is necessary.

Chapter Seven
Pride and Confusion

Man was created the most majestic of God's creatures on the earth. We stand and walk upright, and we were created to rule over the earth and all of its other creatures. We were also created in the image of God. Every human being is marvelous, even to the angels that we were created a little lower than (see Hebrews 2:7). We were created to have a special fellowship with God Himself. God has even chosen to make His dwelling place with man. For these reasons it is easy for man to become proud. However, because of the fall we will also forever have a reason to be humble. God did not cause man to fall—that was man's choice, but it will serve to allow him to be exalted to the high place of being the abode of God, because we will forever have reason to fully understand our need and dependence on His grace and redemption.

Pride is one of the biggest open doors to confusion. As we are told in Proverbs 11:2, **"When pride comes, then comes dishonor, but with the humble is wisdom."** The Hebrew word that is translated "dishonor" here is *qalown* (kaw-lone'), which is also translated "disgrace, dishonor, ignominy, reproach, shame, and confusion." These are all consequences of the fall. If we are to walk in the honor and dignity of our calling, we must begin with the humility to know how desperately dependent we are on the grace and redemption of God that is available to us at the cross. To walk in the light and to be able to see where we are going will require humility. We must start to recognize this deadly enemy of pride and repent of it.

We must also begin to demand humility from those we recognize as leaders in the church or we will continue to experience the "disgrace, dishonor, ignominy, reproach, shame, and confusion" that has been the domain of the church for so long now. Leaders lead people to where they are. They impart to those who are under them what is in them. If they are walking in pride the people will end up in pride, and the confusion that it causes.

If we are going to be free from confusion, we must be consistent in our own hearts, which is to walk and live in reality and truth. If you have difficulty in this area, it is likely that you have a problem with confusion. This is important to admit because this acknowledgment can be a big part of the battle to overcome confusion. Obviously I had a problem with it or I would not have had to learn these truths that I am sharing here. This is also important to admit because doing so will begin to break the power of one of the most powerful entryways of confusion—pride. Therefore, James 4:6-8 is a crucial truth in this battle against confusion, as well as in our overall pursuit of God.

...Therefore it says, "GOD is opposed to the proud, but gives grace to the humble."

Submit therefore to God. Resist the devil and he will flee from you.

Draw near to God and He will draw near to you. Cleanse your hands, you sinners; and purify your hearts, you double-minded.

The main reason we usually refuse to acknowledge a problem is pride, which is the pride that will even cause God to resist us. As Peter Lord likes to say, "The main thing is to keep the main thing the main thing," and the main thing we need in our life is God's grace. Since He gives grace to the humble, pursuing humility is one of the most worthwhile devotions we can have.

Many of the complications in people's lives are the direct result of pride. For this reason, in many cases confusion will start to dispel the moment we determine to humble ourselves in a matter. When we catch this truth, as well as the even more important one that God gives His grace to the humble, we will begin to spend more time seeking to humble ourselves than trying to exalt ourselves. This alone can send great clouds of darkness fleeing. Those who start to know the true value of the grace and favor of God will not care at all what they look like before people—their pursuit will be the grace of God that comes with humility. In fact, as this truth becomes reality to us, we will start devoting more time to looking smaller, trying to humble ourselves at every opportunity.

As the verses above also reveal, humbling ourselves is how we submit to God and resist the devil. Pride caused the first fall, the fall of the devil himself, and it has caused most of the falls from grace since. Therefore, whenever we humble ourselves we are submitting to God and resisting the devil at the same time. When we start doing this the devil will flee from us because he knows that we are about to receive the grace and favor of the Lord that is directly convertible into the spiritual currency of spiritual authority.

Just being a Christian in this world requires a certain amount of humility. The pride that most of the people of this world live by promotes the ideas that belief in God is a crutch. I fully agree with this because I know

I need a crutch. In fact, at the end of this age things will be in such a mess that all of humanity and the rest of creation, will know for sure that we cannot run things without God—we need Him! I thank Him daily that He is willing to be our crutch!

The same is true of all men whether they acknowledge it or not. Not one of us could even draw a breath without His grace. The greatest genius may be an atheist, but he would not be a genius without the abilities that God gave to them. Pride in our own mental abilities gives an opening to the most base and ridiculous confusion that has come from man or upon man.

For example, if you went for a walk on the beach one morning and found a brand new Mercedes, complete with gas in the tank and manuals in the glove compartment, and someone tried to tell you that the ocean made that car and deposited it on the beach, you would consider them an idiot more on the level of an oyster than a human being. Even so, that is exactly the kind of ridiculous theories that naturalists have tried to compel modern men to believe—and most modern men have swallowed it!

Consider this, the extensive, sequential knowledge in the DNA of *a single living cell* is far more complex than what was required to make the Mercedes. For the ocean to have produced a single living cell would be a greater miracle than if it had created this car, with the gas, keys, manuals, and everything else in it! However, even the most dull among us would have trouble believing that the ocean even created a tire that we found on the beach—how can we go on believing the kind of foolishness that naturalists are proposing? However, naturalists are trying to convince the world that not only a living cell came from the ocean, but zillions of similar miracle accidents, all in perfect timing, took place to develop life as we know it without a single mishap—and all of this happened by accident!

For these "brilliant scientists" to believe the foolishness that naturalism promotes can only be attributed to confusion of the highest level. How could they day after day observe the miracles of creation, and then freely admit that the power of all our computers combined is still not enough to even compute the odds that just one of the miracles could happen by itself and still believe that this all happened by accident, unless they are under one of the darkest clouds of confusion? Even the most simple observer in honest natural science will conclude that there was a Superior Intelligence far beyond anything we can yet even begin to measure that brought forth all that we know—therefore there had to be a Creator.

The pride of man in such forms as humanism is the source of some of the darkest forms of confusion on the earth. It was a nationalistic pride that led some of the world's most noble and brilliant people, the Germans, to fall to the tragic delusions of the Nazis. Such pride will open the door to delusions in our churches, our companies, and even our families. Any good that we are or have which is not acknowledged as being the grace of God will be a wide open door for delusion and deception.

Chapter Eight
Sin and Confusion

We have already superficially covered the source of confusion, but we need to look at it in more depth to close this major source of confusion into our lives. As stated, there is some repetition throughout this study (by design). There are also overlaps and interrelationships between the sources of confusion that merit the review of some of these principles.

As stated, the first thing the serpent did to cause Adam and Eve to sin is to get them to question the clear commandment of God. Then he tried to get them to question God's intentions. This is still one of the devil's most effective strategies in causing God's people to stumble—blur the commandment, and then get us to rationalize God's intention for giving it. Just giving in to this line of thinking can open the door wide for confusion to enter our lives.

The devil dwells in darkness. That is his domain. For him to bring us into bondage under his domain he must first cloud our vision, and then darken it. Getting us to compromise the clear mandates of God is the primary way that he does this, and it will always lead to our bondage to the devil and his ways.

Martin Luther once made an interesting statement. He said, "If you sin, sin boldly!" He was not encouraging people to willfully sin. He was encouraging them to call sin "sin" and not to try to rationalize it. If you rationalize it you will never repent of it.

When we sin we usually go through the same process that Adam and Eve did after their sin. First we try to hide. Then we try to blame shift. Adam declared that it was the woman's fault, and the woman tried to blame the serpent. This only adds to our confusion. The only way out of the confusion, which is the result of sin, is to repent of the sin. To repent you have to acknowledge that you did something wrong. God does not forgive excuses—He forgives sin. He will forgive our sin as we acknowledge and repent of it. To be free we must stop trying to hide our sin and stop trying to justify it—we must repent.

Do not ever allow the devil to get you to start compromising the clear Word of the Lord. You will always be much better off if you do not do what you know is wrong but if you sin, as Martin Luther encouraged, be honest about it. For many people this one thing can so dramatically deliver them from the confusion in their lives that it is like turning a hurricane into a bright sunny day.

If Adam and Eve had run to God instead of trying to hide from Him and blame shift, the whole world would probably be a far less dark and violent place than it is today. They would have still died, and we would still need the atonement of the cross, but it would not have been *as bad.* My point is that there are always bad consequences for sin and we cannot escape them, but we can lessen them. We will always be much better off if we run to God when we sin instead of away from Him. He will forgive us and cover the sin if we repent of it. As we read earlier in I John 1:9-10:

> **If we confess our sins, He is faithful and righteous to forgive us our sins and to cleanse us from all unrighteousness.**
>
> **If we say that we have not sinned, we make Him a liar, and His word is not in us.**

One of the ways that the devil is trying to prepare the world for his "deep darkness" is to blur distinctions, because when something is distinct it is clear. Let's look at the distinctions between men and women. The Lord made men and women different so they would need each other, not so they would be in perpetual conflict. Our differences compliment each other, causing us to fit together so that it takes both to make a whole. However, I will never be able to become one with my wife by making her into a man. To become one I must recognize and appreciate the way the Lord made us different.

One of the main social reasons why there is such a drive to blur the distinctions between men and women, and to refuse other forms of stereotyping, is because this has often been used to wrongly discriminate against a people group. The differences between men and women, or between races, nations, and cultures, should not be a cause for wrongful discrimination, but to refuse to recognize the differences is to be blind to reality. Though justice is often portrayed as being blind, true and ultimate justice will never come from blindness, but from acknowledgment of truth and reacting to it with justice in our heart.

There are similar movements to blur the distinctions between good and evil and different religions saying such things as— "we all worship the same god." These statements and ideas are not true, and though we should show dignity and respect for all people who are made in the image of God, the god served by any other religion is not our same God.

It was by trying to serve other gods simultaneously with Jehovah that the Israelites repeatedly fell into confusion and bondage, and were ultimately driven from their Promised Land. If we begin to compromise the One we serve for the sake of peace or being accepted by other people, we are in fact denying the One we claim to serve and opening ourselves to the ultimate deception and confusion. The ultimate sin is to deny our God and worship other gods.

In Amos 3:3 it is asked, **"Can two walk together, unless they are agreed?"** (NKJV). This is an important question, but one that is often misunderstood. Many have interpreted it to mean that we cannot walk with anyone unless we are in perfect agreement with them. If we carry that to its logical conclusion no human being would ever be able to have any kind of relationship with another human being. What this verse does mean is that we can walk together with others in the things that we do agree on.

For example, I recognize the profound difference between Islam and Christianity. However, I do have more in common with one who at least believes in God than I do with an atheist. I could very easily join with Muslims or those of other religions to protect religious liberty. I would "walk together" with them in pursuing or protecting the freedom of worship. However, I would not to any degree compromise the fact that there is only one true God—Jesus is His Son, and no one can come to God except through the atonement made by the Son. I would not worship with anyone who did not believe these basics.

Among Christians we should be able to walk together in more areas, but not necessarily in everything. If we would walk together in the things that we do agree on, we would probably start to trust each other enough to at least listen to views on things that we may not agree on. When we do this we will usually find that our positions and beliefs are not as far apart as we may have thought, and soon we are more open to hearing from each other. Often we will discover that though we may still disagree it is not as big a deal as we may have made of it.

However, to avoid opening the door to confusion we should never compromise our convictions for the sake of unity, and we will never need to do this for true unity. One of the basic characteristics of true humility is to be teachable. To be teachable is to be open and willing to learn, but that does not mean to compromise. We should always be humble enough to change our convictions when we are clearly shown that they are wrong, but to never compromise them. To compromise is to surrender a position for the sake of political expediency, which will be the basis of false unity at best. To compromise the truth is also sin, and it will open the door to confusion. The basic commodity that our lives as Christians are built on is truth.

Chapter Nine

Spiritual Attacks and Confusion

Another main source of confusion among Christians is simply spiritual attack. We can allow inroads of an evil spirit of confusion by our disobedience. But Christians can also suffer attacks from a spirit of confusion which is the result of them doing what is right, not what is wrong. However, these attacks can be easily distinguished and resisted. As we are delivered from confusion and walk in the path of the righteous, which has ever increasing light, we will more quickly discern the source of confusion, and be able to shut that gate of hell through which it is coming.

As we acknowledge I Corinthians 14:33, **"for God is not a God of confusion but of peace..."** We should not have confusion, but rather the peace of God in our lives, which will dispel the confusion. God never uses confusion against His people, and no confusion that His people suffer ever comes from Him. Therefore, confusion should not be the normal state of any Christian. This does not mean that Christians will not have trials and get attacked with confusion, but it is never coming from God, so we must resist it until it flees.

This also does not mean that we will not go through periods when we are not sure which direction to take, or what decision to make in a matter. However, there is a difference between not being sure about something yet, and being in confusion about it.

If confusion is the result of an attack from the enemy, just discerning it will begin to dispel it. Remember, the enemy dwells in darkness because his main power is the power of deception. So, every time we shine the light on him or his work, it begins to break his power. Then, as soon as we begin to resist him he will flee. If confusion is the result of our own mistakes or sin, we must recognize and repent of them so the gate that confusion is using to gain access into our lives can be closed. If it is the result of allowing the fear of man to control us, we must repent of making men idols in which we have put our trust and hope, instead of God. If it is the result of a spiritual attack we must recognize it and resist the devil until he flees.

The spirit of confusion is an enemy of truth and light, and is a thief that has come to steal our life. The spirit of confusion will try to rob us of our very purpose for being here. To be free of confusion we must determine to live within the peace and joy that mark the borders of the kingdom of God. We must resolve that we will not allow ourselves to be distracted from the domain of our God for a single day, so we will not be drawn into the enemy's domain of darkness.

As stated, for various reasons everyone will have to deal with confusion from time to time, and it does not necessarily mean that a demonic spirit is attacking us every time we get confused about something. However, Christians are called to abide in Christ, not in confusion. Again, we should consider any confusion as an alarm that something is not right, and it needs to be put right.

A growing source of spiritual confusion in our times is witchcraft. As we have published much on the subject of witchcraft, including a booklet in this same Stronghold Series, we will only touch on it briefly here, borrowing from the previous work.

The practice of witchcraft has dramatically increased throughout the world in recent years. One of the expressed goals of this movement is to dilute, subjugate, and destroy biblical Christianity. Many Christians are presently suffering attacks in some form from those who practice witchcraft. Discerning the nature of these attacks and knowing how to overcome them is becoming crucial for all believers.

We are exhorted not to be ignorant of the enemy's schemes (see II Corinthians 2:11). Peter warned us, saying, **"Be of sober spirit, be on the alert. Your adversary, the devil, prowls about like a roaring lion, seeking someone to devour. But resist him, firm in your faith..." (I Peter 5:8-9)**. Understanding Satan's schemes significantly increases our advantage in the battle. The entire church age has been one of spiritual warfare which is increasing as we approach the end of the age. Those who refuse to acknowledge the reality of this warfare and therefore do not fight are being overcome. Every Christian is living behind enemy lines. Presently, the whole world does lie in the power of the evil one. We are here to destroy his works—we are here to fight!

Satan is now being cast out of the heavenlies and down to the earth where he is coming with great wrath. This is the reason for the increasing confusion upon the earth among nations. Even so, we need not fear— He who is in us is much greater than he who is in the world. He who is least in the kingdom of God has more power than any anti-Christ. But just as the greatest military power today is vulnerable if it does not recognize the enemy's attack, we too are vulnerable if we do not recognize Satan's schemes. The only way he can defeat us is by our own ignorance or complacency. As we maintain our position in Christ, take on the full armor of God and remain vigilant, we will not only stand but we will prevail against the gates of hell.

What Is Witchcraft?

Witchcraft is counterfeit spiritual authority; it is using a spirit other than the Holy Spirit to dominate, manipulate, or control others.

The apostle Paul named witchcraft or "sorcery" as one of the works of the flesh in Galatians 5:20. It has its origin in the carnal nature though it usually degenerates quickly into demonic power. Trying to use emotional pressure to manipulate others is a basic form of witchcraft. Using hype or soul power to enlist service, even for the work of God, is witchcraft. Businessmen scheming to find pressure points while pursuing a deal may also be using witchcraft. Many of the manipulative tactics promoted as sales techniques in marketing are basic forms of witchcraft. Recognizing them, and refusing to use them, is repentance that begins to enable us to be trusted with true spiritual authority.

The basic defense against counterfeit spiritual authority is to walk in true spiritual authority. Establishing our lives on truth, and trusting in the Lord to accomplish what concerns us, are both essential if we are going to be free of the influence and pressure of witchcraft.

It is written that Jesus is seated upon the throne of David. This is of course a metaphor as David established a position of true spiritual authority that would ultimately issue in the kingdom of God. David did for spiritual authority what Abraham did for faith. How did David establish a seat of true authority? Basically he refused to take authority or influence for himself, but completely trusted in God to establish him in the position that He had ordained for him.

Any authority, which is influence that we gain by our own manipulation or self-promotion, will be a stumbling block to us and our ability to receive a true commission and authority from God. If we are going to walk in true spiritual authority, like David, we will have to trust in the Lord to establish us in it, and in His time. As Peter exhorted, **"Humble yourselves, therefore, under the mighty hand of God,** *that He may exalt you at the proper time"* (I Peter 5:6 emphasis mine).

Witchcraft is rooted in the profound pride whereby one begins to think that he should be the one in control, and that he has the wisdom and should have the power to enforce his will on others. This is the end result of the most basic rebellion against God and His leadership. Therefore every true spiritual leader who is appointed by God will have a healthy humility whereby he knows that he cannot accomplish what is right without God. He will abhor the thought of doing things in his own wisdom or strength. Those who are self-appointed, or who have fallen from a right relationship with God, will be exposed by their pride and arrogance in leadership.

We discussed earlier in Proverbs 11:2 that, **"When pride comes, then comes dishonor, but with the humble is wisdom"** and that the Hebrew word translated "dishonor" is also translated "disgrace, dishonor, ignominy, reproach, shame, and confusion." Are these not all of the things that the church has consistently and repeatedly been subject to? We can trace all of this back to when leadership in the church was made into a position of privilege and power over others instead of the place of service by servant leaders that it was intended to be.

We will continue to see the church subject to the reproach and the resulting confusion until we do what the Lord commanded the Ephesian Church to do in Revelation 2:2: **"...put to the test those who call themselves apostles, and they are not..."** We might paraphrase this to say "put to the test those who claim to be sent by God and are not." This also implies that we should reject them as our leaders. These "false apostles" will be evidenced by their pride, which will always ultimately lead to dishonor and confusion. Because these are counterfeit spiritual authorities, we can expect such to use the counterfeit spiritual authority of manipulation, control, and other schemes to accomplish their purposes. We must reject such as these or we will pay the ultimate price of confusion.

Chapter Ten

Other Sources of Confusion

In this chapter we are going to very briefly look at other sources of confusion that are revealed in Scripture.

Unrighteous Judgment

Isaiah 59:4 states, **"No one sues righteously and no one pleads honestly. They trust in confusion, and speak lies; they conceive mischief, and bring forth iniquity."** By this we see that there will be confusion when there is evil intent or attempts to plead our case by anything but straightforward honesty. When we try to manipulate others in this way we open our own lives to the same.

This verse is especially addressing lawsuits. Some Christians believe that they should never sue because of I Corinthians 6:5-8,

> **I say this to your shame. Is it so, that there is not among you one wise man who will be able to decide between his brethren,**
>
> **but brother goes to law with brother, and that before unbelievers?**

Actually, then, it is already a defeat for you, that you have lawsuits with one another. Why not rather be wronged? Why not rather be defrauded?

On the contrary, you yourselves wrong and defraud, and that your brethren.

First, it was not the apostle's intention here to condemn all lawsuits. Lawsuits were a basic part of the system of justice that God had established in Israel. He was protesting that they were taking their suits before unbelieving judges because there were no trustworthy judges among the believers.

Paul was also saying to the Corinthians that there was a higher way which was to forgive and accept the wrong. This is what Jesus did when He went to the cross knowing that He could have demanded justice and called on legions of angels to come to His aid. Even so, Paul obviously understood that there are times when one must sue for justice, even before unbelievers, which is what he himself actually did when he sued for justice by appealing to Caesar. However, in his case against the rulers of Israel who were trying to kill him, there was no possibility of going before believers to resolve the matter.

In I Corinthians 6, Paul illuminates what is certainly one of the greatest causes of shame in the body of Christ today—the fact that there are no judges in the church. We are told in Psalm 89:14, **"Righteousness and justice are the foundation of Thy throne..."** Even though we have not been doing very well with the righteousness part, it is very rare to even hear of justice being addressed in the church—and justice is one of the two foundational pillars of the Lord's throne. If we are going to live in the kingdom, under the authority of the King, we must have both righteousness and justice established in the church.

The New Testament church government was typed after the model of Israel's biblical government. A foundation for that government was established through Moses, and was further developed through Joshua and the Judges after they had entered their Promised Land, in preparation for the age of the kings which was to be a biblical model for the kingdom.

From the beginning, the foundation of the civil authority in Israel was established on the recognition of elders. One of the primary duties of the elders was to sit in the gates of the cities and act as judges for the people. Likewise, this is actually supposed to be one of the primary functions of elders in the church. Paul was lamenting to the Corinthians that they did not have anyone who was actually functioning in this way. Not having this foundation of "justice" established in the church is probably a major reason why the Corinthians were also having some serious problems in the area of righteousness as well. God's throne, or His authority, will always be built on both of the pillars of righteousness and justice, together.

Today it seems that the universal church is in the same condition that the Corinthians were, having no judges and therefore experiencing continual shame and confusion. This is a subject worthy of study in itself and cannot be fully dealt with here, but it is easy to see that it remains a wide open door for confusion in the church just as it was in Corinth.

Gathering Without a Purpose

An example of this is found in Acts 19:32, **"So then, some were shouting one thing and some another, for the assembly was in confusion, and the majority did not know for what cause they had come together."**

I have been in some very wonderful meetings in which people came together without an agenda, just open for the Lord to move in a unique way. However, for every one of these meetings in which I experienced a move of the Holy Spirit, there were dozens that ended up in confusion. I have come to the conclusion that if the mature do not take the authority that has been given to them, the immature, rebellious, and confused will seize the opportunity to fill the void.

I do believe that it can be a worthy goal for prayer meetings, home groups, or even churches, to come to the place of spiritual maturity where they are completely open to the Spirit to move in their gatherings. However, the key word here is that this can be a worthy "goal." You do not climb a mountain by jumping right to the top—there is a step-by-step ascent. To try to do this with immature believers is opening the door wide to confusion in our meetings.

There is good as well as bad control. Of course, to the rebellious, stubborn, or self-willed, any restraint will be considered a "control spirit." Even so, without the good control the chaos and confusion in this world would be unbearable. My younger children require much more control and oversight than my older children. It should be this way in the church as well. As a church matures it should need less restraints. However, if there is true life in a church it will have a continual influx of new believers who will need a lot of oversight and control in their lives while they mature. If you just throw the meetings open to being "led by the Spirit" you are likely to be led by a spirit you do not want to be lead by—confusion.

One who gets the mind of the Lord before a meeting and is able to steer it in the right way is just as much being led by the Spirit as one who claims to be led spontaneously. In fact, it was the nature of the Lord to see the end from the beginning, so it seems that those who are truly maturing in Him should be able to get His mind for a meeting beforehand. A key is to remain humble and flexible enough to always be aware that we "see in part" and "know in part." There are probably parts to the meeting that God would also like to include which we may not be aware of beforehand, so we should remain open to these.

For the sake of avoiding much frustration and confusion we should always have a purpose for our gatherings. Although we always want to be sensitive to the Spirit as well as flexible, generally we should have the leadership and discipline to follow through with that purpose.

Prophesying Out of Order

Confusion can be the result of prophets prophesying out of order. In I Corinthians

14:31-33 we read, **"For you can all prophesy one by one, so that all may learn and all may be exhorted; and the spirits of prophets are subject to prophets; for God is not a God of confusion but of peace, as in all the churches of the saints."**

First we see here that **"you can all prophesy."** The Lord can use anyone at anytime to prophesy. In fact, because we "see in part" and "prophesy in part" we will need to have more than one person prophesying if we are going to get the complete message.

We also see here that **"the spirits of the prophets are subject to the prophets."** This means that if anyone prophesying loses control of themselves, it is their fault! I have heard people say the Spirit just took over the mind and tongue to give the message through them, or even took over their bodies to make them do strange things as a part of the message, but this is evidence that another spirit other than the Holy Spirit was involved. The **"spirits of the prophets are subject to the prophets,"** because as this text declares, **"God is not a God of confusion."** Confusion, which is the result of a message that did not come from the Holy Spirit, but rather from another spirit, will be the result if we lose control of our own spirits.

Jealousy, Selfish Ambition, and Confusion

The following text from James 3:11-18 is one of the most important in the Bible for establishing a basic grid for discernment:

> **Does a fountain send out from the same opening both fresh and bitter water?**
>
> **Can a fig tree, my brethren, produce olives, or a vine produce figs? Neither can salt water produce fresh.**
>
> **Who among you is wise and understanding? Let him show by his good behavior his deeds in the gentleness of wisdom.**
>
> **But if you have bitter jealousy and selfish ambition in your heart, do not be arrogant and so lie against the truth.**
>
> **This wisdom is not that which comes down from above, but is earthly, natural, demonic.**
>
> **For where jealousy and selfish ambition exist, there is disorder [confusion] and every evil thing.**
>
> **But the wisdom from above is first pure, then peaceable, gentle,**

reasonable, full of mercy and good fruits, unwavering, without hypocrisy.

And the seed whose fruit is righteousness is sown in peace by those who make peace.

We see here that where there is **"jealousy and selfish ambition exists there is disorder** [confusion] **and every evil thing."** Jealousy and selfish ambition are two of the widest open doors to confusion and every other kind of evil. **"Every evil thing"** is included here because when confusion comes, you can count on it bringing many of its friends.

So how do we counter this? We counter every evil spirit with the Spirit of Christ. It was His nature to humble Himself, leaving His exalted seat of glory to become a man, living in the most humble circumstances, and even giving His life for our salvation and ultimate exaltation to be heirs of God with Him. He will even allow us to do greater works than He did now that He has returned to the Father. If we really have the Spirit of Christ, it will be most profoundly exhibited by our willingness to humble ourselves to help save and promote others. The true nature of one who is walking in the Spirit of Christ is that the ones we serve will go farther than we did. In a sense, our ceiling will become the floor for those that we raise up.

Contrary to this, we know that Jesus was crucified because of envy. Throughout history most of the strife and divisions in the church are the result of the same—jealousy and selfish ambition. That is why **"the seed whose fruit is righteousness is sown in peace by those who make peace."** There is a peace that abides with those who are not being driven by either jealousy or selfish ambition that imparts peace like seeds wherever they go.

This is further summarized in I John 2:5-6, 9-11, and 3:10-16, 18:

> **but whoever keeps His word, in him the love of God has truly been perfected. By this we know that we are in Him:**
>
> **the one who says he abides in Him ought himself to walk in the same manner as He walked....**
>
> **The one who says he is in the light and yet hates his brother is in the darkness until now.**
>
> **The one who loves his brother abides in the light and there is no cause for stumbling in him.**
>
> **But the one who hates his brother is in the darkness and**

walks in the darkness, and does not know where he is going because the darkness has blinded his eyes...

By this the children of God and the children of the devil are obvious: anyone who does not practice righteousness is not of God, nor the one who does not love his brother.

For this is the message which you have heard from the beginning, that we should love one another;

not as Cain, who was of the evil one, and slew his brother. And for what reason did he slay him? Because his deeds were evil, and his brother's were righteous.

Do not marvel, brethren, if the world hates you.

We know that we have passed out of death into life, because we love the brethren. He who does not love abides in death.

Everyone who hates his brother is a murderer; and you know that no murderer has eternal life abiding in him.

We know love by this, that He laid down His life for us; and we ought to lay down our lives for the brethren

Little children, let us not love with word or with tongue, but in deed and truth.

Our ultimate deliverance from confusion will come when we walk in the perfect love of God, which is to know His love for us, and to be a vessel for Him to use and show His love to others. Love simplifies like nothing else ever will. There is not a higher calling or greater power than the love of God. That is why **"love never fails..."** **(I Corinthians 13:8).**